BLOOM
PUBLICATIONS

Books That Help Kids Bloom & Grow

Copyright © 2022 S. Alston

All rights reserved.
No part of this book may be reproduced
or used in any manner without the prior written
permission of the copyright owner, except for the
use of brief quotations in a book review.

ISBN: 979-8-9869086-0-1 (Hardcover)
ISBN: 979-8-9869086-1-8 (Paperback)

Illustrations by, Kiran Tariq

First Edition, 2022
Bloom Publications

www.bloompublications.com

I AM MIGHTY ME

Mighty Me Series
BOOK 1

NOTE TO PARENTS:

Becoming self-aware is a necessary skill to cultivate if you want to be a creator of your life rather than a victim of life circumstances. By reading the Mighty Me Series™ with your child, you'll be teaching them they have control over their thoughts, feelings, and actions, which empowers them and helps them to feel good about themselves.

Repetition builds strong habits, so you'll improve your child's self-esteem as you continue reading empowering books and encouraging good behavior. Focus on the behavior you want to see rather than drawing too much attention to the behavior you don't want to develop. Let them know they are strong and mighty and that they can choose to use their powers for good!

The more you notice when they are kind and helpful, the faster that grows! Then feel great knowing you have helped unlock the superhero within!

Every day I am growing,
I'm mighty And strong.
When I eat healthy foods,
I feel good all day long.

I love when I'm jumping!
I skip and I hop.
It's fun to play games
and blow bubbles that POP!

Sometimes I sing and
I dance to the beat,
Sometimes I'm quiet,
read books in my seat.

I'm mighty and strong, so I pick up my toys;
like my cars and my blocks and my favorite cowboys.
I make it a game when I put them away,
I finish real quick and have more time to play.

My dog is named Rover and he likes to run.
We play and we walk outside in the sun.

I even help mommy, she cooks for us all.
I set out the plates and I try not to fall.

Feeling proud when I eat all the food on my plate.
Then I'm off to the bathtub before it's too late.

Then I zoom to my room to read books and to say

When I care for my body,
I feel at my best.
So, making good choices
is not a hard test.
And helping my family is
easy you see,
because I am mighty

I AM MIGHTY ME!

WAYS I HELP MY FAMILY

_____

_____

_____

_____

Lightning Source UK Ltd.
Milton Keynes UK
UKHW050614160223
417096UK00003B/14